Pursuance

· ·

A BLESSING

ENHANCE CHANGE, EMPOWER
YOURSELF, DREAM BIG AND BELIEVE
YOU CAN DO IT!!

Jason Curtis Lugo

authorHOUSE®

AuthorHouse™
1663 Liberty Drive
Bloomington, IN 47403
www.authorhouse.com
Phone: 1 (800) 839-8640

Published by AuthorHouse 06/11/2018

ISBN: 978-1-5462-4556-8 (sc)
ISBN: 978-1-5462-4555-1 (hc)
ISBN: 978-1-5462-4554-4 (e)

Library of Congress Control Number: 2018906670

Contents

$\mathcal{F}$oreword

I HAVE THE pleasure of introducing this simple book to you, penned by a simple man Mr. Jason Lugo, Education Specialist (at the Oakland Unified School District) who after insurmountable challenges in his young life, has made it to the pinnacle of success by sheer willpower and constant pursuance. It is just a tip of the iceberg into the life of a "shining star" Jason who I am proud to say is my cousin.

He happens to be the major force behind my tertiary education, where he personally made sure to have me enlisted in the Social work degree programme. He always took it upon himself to enquire as to my progress with full encouragement, until I finally graduated with a Bachelors of Science degree in Social Work from the University of the Sothern Caribbean.

This book was written with the intention of encouraging those who feel that they are unable to overcome the challenges in their lives. Its main focus is in discovering your God given talents and gifts and to vigorously pursue them to reach your full potential.

The readers would be furnished with insights into the writer's real life experiences, and the negative effects upon his young life. Notwithstanding the abject poverty he was faced with, the shame and ridicule from close relatives and friends, the loneliness and low self esteem, Jason drew on his strengths and his deep faith in God, and turned all negative into positives.

This book may help fill the void in so many lives that are yearning for maybe, a word, a sentence, a listening ear, someone who truly care, to steer them towards self awareness and fulfillment. When self awareness materializes, a whole new world will open up and this will automatically lead to serious exploration of your gifts and talents. This book is not an antidote for all challenges that one may face in life, but it will positively impact those who are determined to do better for themselves, to reach their full potential.

At the end of the book there is an appendix with simple questions for you the readers to answer to ascertain exactly where you are in life, how satisfied you are at the level you have reached in your endeavors, and what course of action you intend to take to make it happen for you. The significance of these questions is to lead you to dig deep into your memories and thoughts so that you may be able to identify and reconstruct that which is hindering your progress.

Listra Lugo BSc Social Work
Freeport,
Trinidad and Tobago,
West Indies

Acknowledgement

THIS BOOK IS dedicated to my dearest mother Martha Lugo. I want you to know that I love you and all I ever wanted, was to make you proud. As the only boy for my mother I always strived to be the best child and sibling. Uppermost in my mind and my chief motivating factor was to witness the pride and joy of my mother as I climbed the ladder of success, step by step. It is also dedicated to my adoptive children at South East Port of Spain Secondary School (SEPOSS): Dwane Regis, Kadeen Graham, Tesfa Bowen, Ashland Mohammed, Tsania Charles, Paul Dookwah, Josiah Thongs, Jewel Joseph, Stephen Joshua Linton and my God-daughter

Jada Franklin. Thanks for allowing me to be in your life and in the process I was enriched with experiences and knowledge. For this I say thanks to God; to Him be the glory, great things He has done.

The Beginning

J ASON CURTIS LUGO was born on the 24th of January, 1970, to Martha Lugo. He grew up in a rural village called Tabaquite, in Trinidad (an island in the Caribbean) with his mother, stepfather, siblings and extended family of his grandparents and a cousin. His family's surname Lugo originated from Venezuela and was established in Trinidad by his grandfather Barnabus "Papit" Lugo who married his grandmother Maria Lopez Lugo and settled in the central range in Trinidad. He called his grandparents "grandma" and "grandpa." They were very strong individuals and he appreciated them very much for helping in his development.

When his grandfather migrated from Venezuela to Trinidad he acquired land in Tabaquite where he planted cocoa and coffee. He taught his family to be self-sufficient hence he reared his livestock, namely pigs and chickens, and planted rice, corn and peas. There were all the fruit trees and provision anyone could imagine around the home and the family never needed to purchase these things at the market place. "Grandma's kitchen garden" had all she needed: vegetables and green seasonings that a home in the countryside must have for cooking. He recalled his Grandma cutting her "callaloo bush" behind the house while she sang her favorite Catholic hymn.

His mother Martha was the last girl for her parents. A very helpful girl, she had a very good heart. This quality his mother possessed was a trait that came directly from her mother Maria. His mother was very particular about her son but did not know how to express her feelings. Jason longed for love and affection from his mother and wished for the occasional hug. Martha however could not give what she was not taught. He was given tangible things to substitute for this but it was not what Jason wanted. He wanted both his parents' love and affection. The rest of Jason's family tried to provide the comfort, love and affection he so longed for.

Jason's father and mother separated from his inception and he was skeptical about their relationship. So as a child, he started to ask questions. Hence he longed for his biological father's input in his life but his father was not interested in his upbringing. In fact, whenever he asked his mother where his father was, her response would be, "He is dead." As time passed by Jason often thought about his father and how life would have been if he was present in the home. These thoughts prompted him to become very shy. To make matters worse his mom moved in with her boyfriend and visited the home from time to time. Eventually her boyfriend became his step-father. This situation at home did not substitute what Jason longed for and wanted as a child.

Jason tried his best to avoid conversations about family, especially about fathers, in his household and at school because he was ashamed and embarrassed. He felt lonely and dreamt of a family with both parents and whenever he saw his friends and cousins with their family members, he became jealous. At this stage in Jason's life he felt he was cheated of a good family and felt extremely sad as he recalled.

Childhood "Boos"

G ROWING UP AMONG his siblings and cousins, Jason was the darkest in complexion. As the years went by his skin colour proved to be a sore point with his close relatives. Ethnicity and skin colour were the determining factors of acceptance for his relatives. They had this twisted notion that people with lighter skin and softer hair were considered superior. Hence he was treated differently to his siblings and cousins, who were lighter in complexion. He was ridiculed due to the colour of his skin and whenever there was conflict with his relatives he was called the "black nigger boy."

The Negro race and dark skinned people were considered inferior, by some of the older relatives. They were considered "ugly" and "dunce" and when his cousins were angry with him, they never let him forget it. Jason felt quite isolated amongst his relatives because of this and he had even started to believe them. At this time in his life he started to further withdraw from his relatives and seek acceptance on the outside.

His loneliness and lack of support became stronger. Whenever he tried to forget about how they labeled him as "black nigger boy" they reminded him and did a good job at it too. This was degrading to Jason and he felt that his cousins' words were carbon copies from what their parents had been saying over a long period of time. His self-esteem and worth depreciated even more and it was really taking a toll on him.

Crying and feeling sorry for himself was becoming the everyday norm. He remembered going to bed and crying and asking God why him. His childhood was not pleasant, as he recalled. Jason became reluctant to do things because of what was said to him. His socialization skill diminished and he stayed away from his cousins because he did not want to upset any one of them. He constantly felt alone, by himself he felt alone, in a group, and in a crowd, it was the same feeling this aloneness was always there. This boy called Jason became locked in and did not want to share his feelings with anyone.

He avoided crowds and if he had to be in such surroundings for whatever reason, loneliness was his constant companion. Interaction with people was uncomfortable and it was worse being around strangers because he would preconceive what they thought about him. This was frustrating for Jason and he felt overwhelmed when people were around him. This feeling continued throughout Jason's childhood and he was searching for something to fill that void inside of him. What kept him sane was the prayers he said and the hope for better days to come.

Jason felt awkward and wondered why he had to be born "a black nigger boy." This was a major issue in his teenage life and he felt inundated at times so he would texturize his hair to get it softer and less thick. His dark skin was really a problem, especially when he was among his relatives, so he began using bleaching cream to lighten his complexion so that he could blend in. This issue was deeper than he thought and he remembered his grandmother saying, "Don't bring home any black and hard hair girl here because you will make late-to-school children."

This really took a toll on Jason and he felt pressured. He often wondered if this was a result of colonialism prominent in his country for decades where the darker-skinned people were treated less than the fair-skinned people. This even pushed Jason to go deeper into a shell because he did not feel confident and was not given the attention he needed as a child. This affected Jason's schoolwork and he found himself not excelling at school in his early years.

In primary school, Jason was having real difficulties in obtaining the proper grades in his tests at the end of the week and at the end of the term. Jason had no one to encourage him and assist him in his academics so he ignored his schoolwork and would find himself doing his homework on the steps of his classroom on mornings. He would hustle to complete his homework so he did not do it with care and effort. He did it only because he knew if he did not complete it; his teacher will flog him in front of the whole class. He was afraid of punishment and this compelled him to at least attempt his homework. This practice became a normal routine for Jason and he dreaded doing homework whenever he was given assignments.

His struggle demotivated him further whenever his reports indicated average or a little above average. He had the ability to do very well but he had no motivation to do his school work and his low self-esteem was certainly a contributing factor. He was not an assiduous student but he was sent to school every day, sun or rain, with all his books in his school bag. His mother did not have the opportunity to do well in school hence she insisted that her son have all his books and be in school every day come what may. He had to comply or he would be flogged.

At times, Jason made excuses not to attend school but he was not allowed to do so even if he was genuinely sick. He recalled not wanting to go to school a particular morning because his peers made a mockery of his "bata dog shoes" (low cost shoes). However he was sent to school late, by himself that morning. He was standing by the side of the road when a hearse came up the road and he quickly ran straight back home. Jason was afraid of the dead and stayed away from funerals. He recalled attending three persons funeral in his life as a child and did so only because all his family members had to attend. Of course, his mother flogged him and sent him back to get a taxi. She was serious about him attending school that morning.

Jason got flogged at school and at home and this did not help but instead, pushed him into a more depressive state. So Jason's self-worth was being cemented to the lowest. This caused him to have little or no interaction with his peers, family members and close relatives and it deepened his feelings of unworthiness. Although Jason was experiencing all of this, his teachers believed that he could do better at his schoolwork; hence whenever children were promoted in his class he was always one of the lucky ones to be advance to another level.

Harnessed Talent

TEACHERS AT PRIMARY school level discovered that he was a talented singer, something that he truly loved. He felt that he could become a singer because he was told that he was good at it. His teachers would call upon him to sing and lead in the song sessions at school and for special functions the principal, Mrs. Crona, would call for him to perform and he executed the songs with actions which delighted his audience.

One of his teachers, Mr. Whiteman, believed he had a God given talent, and wrote calypso songs for him to perform at the annual carnival season competitions. Jason vividly remembered his favorite song written by Mr. Whiteman, his Standard Three teacher:

"Ah coming on strong, strong, strong ah coming to take the crown. Tell then judges wait, wait, wait Jason now entering the gate. Ah singing ah sweet, sweet melody and everybody will join with me. Tell them boys beware, ah coming to make a clean sweep this year."

Jason felt real joy whenever he was called upon to

sing and felt appreciated for doing it. He was still shy and it took a lot out of him to execute his songs. This joy he felt on stage and the attention he was given started slowly but surely boosting Jason's self-esteem. He was a natural singer and recalled singing ever since he could have uttered words. He learnt all the songs from the radio and used to practice whenever he could outside the house or in the bathroom. He wanted to become a singer so decided to enter competitions and was successful at them too.

His mother did not believe in this singing talent of his, and although several attempts were made to convince her, she still did not want to hear about it. His mother did not see her son making a success at this career and hence discouraged him in his quest to become a singer. Jason did not give up, though, and he continued learning songs from the radio and whenever his teachers gave him new songs, he continued to lead and perform to his best. This helped Jason to feel better about himself and he started singing in church, where his life began turning around. The more he sang in church and for concerts, the more he would be applauded for it.

Spiritual Insight

JASON'S RELIGION TAUGHT about prayer and how it can change things. Jason relied on God for filling that emptiness he felt. His life became a bit intense and he felt that God was becoming more important so he prayed to become a better person. He sought spiritual upliftment to fill the void in his life. Whenever churches in the community held crusades he would make sure he was present, hungry for God's word. He never missed a night at the crusades and was always eager to learn more about Him. His first Bible was won during a Bible verse competition and he gave his life to Christ that night.

Jason was 10 years old when he recalled making a promise to God. He promised God that he would serve him the rest of his life if he (God) could grant him success at his promotional exams (Common Entrance). That exam was extremely challenging to Jason but he did not want to fail because he would have to face his mother and his relatives with shame. He decided to give his examination a good shot, so he studied hard.

Well, after waiting with great anticipation, his results came and he was indeed successful. He was placed in a five year school in his village: Tabaquite Composite School. He felt elated and was excited for this new adventure in his life.

Jason still struggled with his self-esteem and felt alone among his peers. However, his mother and aunt operated the cafeteria at his new school and he felt compelled to do well at examinations. After his first term Jason felt that he could have done better so he decided to compete with the other members in his class and ended up among the top students the following term.

The first year of his secondary school had come finally to an end and it was time to be assessed for the second year. When he returned to school after the vacation period Jason was surprised to learn that he was placed among the best students in a special class in Form Two. This class was given the best teachers in the school and was a model for years to come. This was the first time this institution had such a dynamic class that was given attention and resources to produce the best students. Of course, the pressure was intense because the best of the best were placed in his class and he needed to prove that he was worthy of such a spot.

Jason was very artistic and he expressed himself in song and visual art, which he was becoming increasingly better at. His art teacher, Mr. Narinesingh, would push him to the limit and encourage him to do better every time. His art work exceeded others in his class and painting with water colours was his favorite expression of imaginary sceneries. He felt good at his work and kept his art work in a safe place in his cupboard at home. But that was not all Jason was interested in at this age; he began a new adventure in analyzing how garments were made. This stemmed from his observation of his godmother's sister sewing. It was fascinating to see how fabric was molded and constructed into a garment to fit a particular figure.

Jason was twelve when he discovered his new

talent and began cutting and constructing garments for himself, such as pajama slacks and shirts. In his spare time at home, Jason gave this new interest much of his attention. He recalled ripping the clothing he wore and estimated and cut new garments with the fabric his mother would buy for her own use. At this time in his life, Jason felt he had a sense of purpose: he felt good about himself creating these garments. After a while he started to master his skill and with the help of a neighbor, Susan "Suzie" David, he learnt to produce his patterns for his apparels as he perfected his skill.

Jason discovered that this gift God bestowed on him was not to be taken lightly and should be shared as a blessing. He worked hard at his gift and in the harnessing process believed that he should become the best in the area. Jason demonstrated how he was becoming a perfectionist, displayed by his product he was producing even at that age and by his dedication and hard work. Something supernatural was happening in his life which he knew and others around him knew also. God was preparing him for greater things, which he was willing to receive and excel at.

At the end of Form Three, Jason knew what he wanted to be and he pushed himself to do the best he could to achieve this. He wanted to be a professional singer, sew his own clothes and in the process help people. At this stage in his life he was more certain that he could be a singer and dreamt about going to the United States of America and becoming a star. The problem was that Jason did not have anyone to help him fulfill his dream so he continued in his limitation to do what he could do to harness his passion for life. He continued learning new songs and singing whenever he was called upon to do so. Jason was now producing his own garments and constructing apparels for his family members, and relatives.

His mother was not pleased with what Jason was venturing into and she did not support him. She continued to discourage him and was uncertain about what her son was going to do with his sewing skills. She would chastise him whenever he took her fabric and made garments and told him to stop using her sewing machine because he would, undoubtedly, break it. This did not stop Jason's determination to perfect his skill. He would cut garments in the day time and at night place the sewing machine in the wardrobe to muffle the sound and sew his garments.

At the end of Form Three, Jason's self-esteem was on a steady incline, so much so that his mother didn't really understand why. His grades in school improved tremendously. Jason remembered distinctly his form teacher's remarks after doing well at his end of term examinations. Mrs. Kalloo clearly stated in her remarks, *"Jason, you can do anything you put your mind to."* Jason took this remark seriously and felt as if he was on top of the world. This motivated Jason to feel good about himself and he began to make strides in his God given talents. His artistic skills were compelling Jason to do well at his school work and build his self-esteem. There was still a lot of work to be done internally but he was at the stage where his life and the people around him had begun to bring purpose to his lost soul.

People were surprised at Jason's new demeanor and he was commended and praised for being positive and persistent. Jason became a favorite among older people and felt that he could have conversed with them much easier than his peers. He got most of his strength from older friends and he was motivated by them. The use of their affirmations and advices were becoming embedded in him and he was further compelled to become someone positive in society: as a child, a sibling in his family and as a positive role model among his peers. He dared to be different and never smoked or drank and he was not pressured to practice delinquency, although at times he felt ostracized by his peers.

Jason's experiences were making him stronger as an individual and he felt that positive people around him were his greatest asset. He did not know that God was preparing him to become the best Jason he could be and his trials were given for this purpose in life. As a teenager he struggled with being lost and rejected but he did not allow his energies to be consumed negatively. They were channeled into his interest. By the end of Form Three, Jason had to choose a career to go alongside his subject choice at the Form Four and Form Five levels at his secondary/high school. Jason felt he needed to continue along both his academic and vocational career paths. The curriculum at the Tabaquite Composite School did not include his choice of technical vocational preferences so he decided to take a transfer to another school which was located far away from where he lived.

Jason did what was needed.

He sought a transfer to the Marabella Senior Comprehensive School and explained to the teachers there about his choice of studies. The transfer form, was signed by his eldest sister Angela. During the August vacation he queried at the school and was told that his transfer had been approved. He was told that he should prepare himself for the upcoming term in September. Jason was excited though; as he prepared himself got his books list and his mother came around and assisted him to get his other school supplies.

Jason got up early every morning for school and traveled by taxi to get there and on evenings, to survive financially for the week; he travelled with the bus and walked the rest of his journey home. This was a sacrifice Jason knew he would have to make because he was warned before he started school by his mother that there would be nothing extra although he was attending a school further from home.

Auntie's Input

O NE OF JASON'S aunt, Auntie Joyce, who made him feel a sense of belonging, invited him to attend her church. She was a Christian and attended the Seventh Day Adventist church in the village. After some hesitation, his mother allowed him to attend the church and on weekends he would journey to his aunt's home. Jason loved going there because he felt loved and a part of her family. So when no one else would invite him to spend holidays he would go to her house.

Jason's spiritual life became stronger and he felt that at this stage he was convicted to be baptized. His mother, however, would not allow him to do so. Jason's family grew up with a strong Catholic influence and they believed that once you were born a Catholic, you must die one. This did not stop Jason so he gave his life to Christ and he really felt that God loved him. Two verses gave Jason strength. John 3:16: "For god so love the world that he give his only begotten son that who so ever believeth in him should not perish but have everlasting life," and Psalms 139:14: I will praise thee; for I am fearfully and wonderfully made: marvelous are thy works; and that my soul knoweth right well." He recited the Bible verses for comfort throughout his teenage life. These were Jason's daily reminder that he was special and he was a unique and gifted child.

Jason's life was becoming daily enriched as he communed with his Father in heaven and he grew stronger spiritually, which was evident in his behavior. His mother recognized her son was changed and Jason would hear his mother relating this to her friends. She could not understand what was happening. It was a family tradition that his mother would take her children to Carnival every year and take pictures. Jason was no longer interested and stayed home alone. Jason used the time alone to explore the Word of God and to discover in-depth wisdom of God. He began writing songs and documenting them. Music was his way of expressing his love for God and he ministered in song whenever he was called upon to do so.

After a while, Jason discovered a new church in the area, and no longer left home to visit his aunt's church. Agape love Chapel came into the area and was founded by Pastor Harvey Argimude and his wife Sister Glenda. This church was small and he felt that he could get more involved so he did, and ministered in song on a regular basis. He did not feel any different serving his God at this church and did not feel any conviction about the doctrine of this new church. The only difference he thought was that the SDA's doctrine mandated that the followers had to honor God on Saturdays, and the Pentecostal church made Sunday a special day to serve the same God. While reading and communing with his God, it was revealed to him that all the days of the week should be kept holy. This was not to be an issue in Jason's life so he settled at Agape Love Chapel on the Guaracara, Tabaquite Road close to where he lived.

Jason's life at home was not smooth and his challenges were becoming difficult. He knew that he had to not only acquiesce to his mother, but his stepfather's wishes as well. Jason felt that the demands of his spirituality and the wishes of his parents were in conflict and he wondered why he was not supported. After all, he was doing what was right to be his best and he knew he was not a delinquent. All of these challenges affected Jason's schoolwork.

Teenage challenges continue to plague his life and to compound it, his immediate family members and close relatives had no encouragement for him. He needed his father even more at this stage. His biological changes and feelings of teenage transition into young adulthood were in progress and he wished that his biological father was around. His focus was his looks and bleaching of the skin became a priority and he exercised on a daily basis to stay fit.

Jason felt he could have pacified his inner feelings by fixing his physical. He found out that thoughts and feelings could not be eradicated in the physical realm. His mind was still swirling around like a roller coaster, all these feelings were still embedded in him and he could not deal with life's challenges alone. His environment reminded him and at times suicidal thoughts came into his mind. Life's everyday challenges became stressful and with the other siblings out of the home he did not have any one to talk to. His pastor became that father figure and he would relate his problems to him. His parents felt that church was a distraction rather than a helpful agent in his life. However, Jason felt that if he gave up church to please his parents he would not be left with any sense of belonging and purpose in his life. This was a hurdle that Jason had to overcome and he knew that the only way he could, was to pray about it.

Jason left home to reside at his sister's home and hoped that it would help him focus on his schoolwork and get away from home. This did not help. He did not feel comfortable there and his school work suffered. He did not do well at his final high school examinations and it became a challenge to get a decent job. After several failed attempts, he felt compelled to continue his schooling part time. Jason eventually achieved academically after several attempts. His skill and talent intrinsically motivated him and the words of his form teacher at high school, that he can do whatever he put his mind to, helped Jason to "will" himself to succeed and push himself further in life. His spirituality further cemented, those words in the depth of his mind "what he could be and do, whatever he put his mind to do". He knew that he had to prove himself to do better than those close relatives who kept 'looking down' on him. He had to acquire a good job.

Jason prayed for God to open doors, if it is His will. He started singing at weddings and special occasions and continued at church and felt good about his talent, his gift. He felt that it was not a gift but was a ministry that he was bestowed with. He felt that through singing, people were touched and convicted and this was evident when people approached him and conveyed this message. He felt good about this gift God gave him and was willing to continue for the love of God.

Divine Encounters

J ASON WAS A proactive child and constantly sought information on different courses and jobs. He applied for a special job, offered by the government of Trinidad and Tobago, The National

Population Census for the country. He waited anxiously for a response. Eventually he received a response for that particular job one afternoon and discovered that the morning of that said day was the interview. Being a persistent and determined individual, Jason journeyed to the main office which was located in the capital of Trinidad which is Port of Spain. After inquiring about his quest for employment, he was told that another interview was scheduled the following week. So he returned the following week and was interviewed. He was told that he needed to purchase the newspaper for results and see if he was chosen. While on his way back home Jason said he was compelled to query about a course he had previously applied for and was not successful. Jason, in his prayer, specifically asked God to open a door for him to attend school if it's his will. Unknown to Jason, he never knew that this was going to be a new beginning and it would accelerate his life.

At the John S. Donaldson Technical Institute, peculiar encounters began with the registrar clerk and then were sent to the head of the department. John S. Donaldson Technical Institute was considered to be a high ranked institution. Students who did well in the secondary school often attended this school in Trinidad and Tobago. The office administrator, Mrs. White (the head of the dept) looked at him with no hesitation and said, "Young man, if the teacher approve of you, I will accept you." He was then sent to the teacher, Mr. Phillip. The teacher said, "My class started six months ago which you tried and were not successful." He paused and said, "What you want me to do? I do not know your abilities." He continued, "The class is about to prepare for exams," and after hesitation he said, "I can test you. Tell me which day you will like to be tested." He said, "You can come back Friday if you want?"

Jason felt that he was not ready and did not know

what was going to be tested but he told him he would come back Friday.

While going down the steps from where the teacher's class was, he felt compelled to do the test. He ran back to the teacher's class and asked him if he could test him today.

Mr. Phillip said, "I am going on lunch. You will have to wait until after lunch."

Jason responded, "I will wait sir".

After two hours, the teacher returned and called him into his classroom while his other students were in session. He gave him a written test, practical and oral tests. These tests were based on the garment construction specialization in tailoring course via the National Examination counsel of Trinidad and Tobago.

After he corrected the test he smiled and said to Jason, "You know I am impressed, I will accept you full time in my class."

This was a dream that Jason wanted. He visualized

himself going to school at this institution. Jason did not know how it was going to happen but he pursued it and eventually it came to pass. He was then told that he had to come back the following week to be interviewed by the principal.

Jason of course went to his interview with the principal the following week.

The principal looked at him and said, "Young man, who made the garments you are wearing?"

Boastfully Jason responded, "I did sir!"

The principal took his pen and signed the paper on his desk and stamped it with the school stamp and said. "Welcome and good luck in your studies sir. You can start tomorrow."

After witnessing what took place, Jason left the office of the principal happy and hurried home to let his mother know. He knew it was the hands of God working and was showing him that his word was coming to light…1 John 5:14-15 "And this is the confidence that we have toward him, that if we ask anything according to his will he hears us. And if we know that he hears us in whatever we ask, we know that we have the requests that we have asked of him."

Jason left home after an altercation with his stepfather and stayed at the Richards' family home at Palmiste. The Richards were close friends to Jason's family but were considered family. Both his big sister Angela and the eldest daughter of the Richards Yvonne were very close. This brought both families together. Jason travelled by bus for a while and for his final year his mother decided to rent a room for him in the city close to school. He stayed at the Salvation Army hostel for men on Henry Street, Port of Spain.

Jason recalled getting a fever the first night in the cold room in that wooden building. Jason had chosen the cheapest room at the time at the hostel because he did not want to financially burden his mother. The environment was not what he had expected

JASON CURTIS LUGO

and eventually he asked to be moved to the concrete building, where he felt safer.

His journey to become independent and self-sufficient was well on the way. He was responsible for cooking, doing his laundry and running his affairs with no family member or friend to assist. This helped Jason to mature faster than he thought he would. Jason at this stage longed for his mother's cooking and appreciated her efforts and caring attributes. His time management skills were harnessed as he had to balance his chores and school work.

The Salvation Army Hostel was an eye opener to Jason. He thought that he was going into an environment that was safe but he soon discovered that individuals who stayed there were using drugs and others prostituted their bodies while others stole for a living. Jason witnessed his other roommates smoking, drinking, and sniffing coke on the compound. His environment was unsafe and when he did his laundry,

42

he had to sit and watch his clothes and shoes dry to ensure that the other tenants didn't steal his belongings.

Jason longed for a friend to talk to and did not see it fit to befriend the tenants at this place he called home. He was the only one going to school there and at times he felt stressed but kept his focus, which was to pass his exams and graduate. This was Jason's major goal and this he did with distinction.

Jason graduated with an overall "A" certificate and that same year was crowned Mr. John S. Donaldson Technical Institute 1991. His singing talent together with the apparel he wore and intelligence wowed the judges at the Institute's annual competition. Jason's self-esteem now was even higher and he continued to strive for excellence and work hard to become the best he could to make his family proud.

Jason got himself into positive activities and never forgot to give thanks to his God, who kept him sane. At this period Jason's loneliness was unbearable, but he occupied his time with positive people and church group activities. After graduation Jason started A-levels on evenings at Queen's Royal College via Polytechnic (sixth form) Evening program and got involved in a choir that practiced at the school called Chanteur Immortal. This was conducted by June Williams Thorne at the time. This kept Jason occupied while he searched for a job. Jason found a home church eventually on Duke Street called the Pentecostal cathedral, so during the week he kept himself busy with different activities.

Throughout the week he was involved with the church: youth ministry, choir and ministering (through singing) Sunday morning practice all kept him motivated while he grew ingrained spiritually. God was Jason's cornerstone and his self-esteem grew while he encouraged others around him to follow their dreams, to become the greatest that God intended them to be. This kept Jason out of trouble which was witnessed on a daily basis with others in his environment as he ventured from the place called home to his different activities within the city of Port of Spain.

Jason applied for several jobs but his dream job was to become a teacher so he applied and waited for response from the Ministry of Education. He never gave up and he continued to search for a job until eventually his first job came as a stitcher/machine operator for a small business owner in Port of Spain. He was paid on a weekly basis according to pieces of garment he constructed. He left the Salvation Army hostel and got a room to rent closer to work from a member of the church he attended. This area was a depressed area but it suited his pocket and he made it work keeping in mind that better days would come. As he passed through the village seeing young men and women wasting their time, he continued to remind himself, never conform to that behavior and that God wants the best for him.

Jason continued his classes and kept active in

church and developed a positive mindset. He was an inspiration to younger people and those he encountered through his life journey. He encouraged his family members, friends and strangers to pursue what their heart desired and gave them advice on how to go about their dreams. Sometimes he would go out of his way to help others in order for them to become industrious and better people. He felt good helping others and would do it expecting nothing in return.

Jason was determined to never give up although at times he had no food to eat and he would drink water and sleep. This was a result of his job being slow and his boss not being able to pay him for his services. He recalled that although he went through those trying times, he never questioned God and knew things would get better.

Jason decided that he wanted to migrate to the United States of America and may eventually pursue his singing career. But God had a different plan for him. He was about to go through the process to leave when he got a letter from the Ministry of Education for him to take up a position as a Technical Vacation Teacher post, at the Bourgh Malatress Secondary School on the Saddle Road in Santa Cruz. This was another time God had really showed his faithfulness to Jason. This was what Jason dreamt doing while he attended the Marabella Senior Comprehensive Secondary School, mentored by his teacher Mr. Percy John. To him God knew what he was doing and so Jason started his journey as a teacher and was determined to be the best in his field.

As a teacher and his genuine interest in others, Jason discovered that the students who were sent to him were not academically inclined so they were placed in these technical vocational classes. This was ironic for principals to do because this course was a specialized course and students were supposed to be at a certain level to pass all the subjects in order to acquire a certificate. Jason did not complain and argue (Philippians 2:14 –"Do everything without complaining or arguing"). Instead, he decided to try his best to motivate these students and to advocate that they would be treated fairly and be given a well-rounded education. These students were given the same examination that matured and well-structured technical institutes students did. This was Jason's challenge and he decided to motivate his students by teaching by demonstration and breaking up the syllabus into realistic practices.

Jason was being tossed from school to school as the youngest in this field of specialization. He would liaise with his students' teachers and would advise the supportive subject teachers to concentrate on areas of interest to coincide with topics being taught in the tailoring class. This was done on a continual basis and he advocated for team teaching in this aspect in the technical and vocational areas.

He applied for a teacher's scholarship to be trained and certified as a technical and vocational teacher and was accepted. This was another door God had opened for him because teachers were not accepted so early to the programme since he had just started teaching. Senior teachers were given the preference and junior teachers had to wait a long time before accessing the diploma programme.

While he pursuing studies in the programme he still had to teach his classes on a day to day basis. He was released on Thursdays to attend his classes at the John S. Donaldson Technical Institute Teachers Wing. This was stressful because the work given on one day was compact for a whole week's students' load.

This programme duration was two years and Jason knew he was not going to fail any subjects at his diploma certification. But while he was studying and teaching at the Chaguanas Senior Comprehensive School he was sent to Fyzabad Composite Secondary

School. This school is located in the deep southern range in Trinidad and it took two and a half hours to and from the school. He continued to advocate for his students and when injustice was inflicted on his students, he would support them. Jason was known to be a proactive teacher and he voiced his plight with force and conviction.

At that school he even studied and wrote exams in two subjects in order to motivate his students. It worked and so he would insist that they all go to class and he checked on his students to see if they were attending the supported subject classes. He stressed on the importance of all the subjects his students were doing and helped them in the other subject areas so they could understand topics.

Jason delighted in helping his students and did not see them as being a burden to him but he always thought about what our next generation should be like, hence his involvement with the students. As a form teacher, he called in parents to deal with issues right away and monitored cases to ensure that students were dealt with appropriately. He took it upon himself to schedule parents meetings to deal with student affairs, ensuring that parents contribution were needed or at least to make parents aware that their children needed their support.

Education And Its True Meaning

JASON CONTINUED TO try and was determined to achieve his goals in life. The traveling was becoming a bit stressful to do both work and study. Jason was transferred to his *Alma Mata*, (high school), Marabella Senior Comprehensive School. So he studied while working at that school. He felt that his contribution to the next generation and his country Trinidad was invaluable. So with great anticipation he worked hard at influencing and motivating the next generation to be industrious citizens. He wanted to institute positive change in the lives of his students and people he came in contact with. This in itself caused Jason to work harder on himself so that he could be a model to his students. Jason graduated in 2002 and was awarded a distinction certification in teacher training.

Jason felt compelled to continue studying but his area of interest shifted after his experiences as a teacher has sensitized him to human behavior. He believed that if he could reach the minds of individuals he could further make a greater contribution to society and his country of Trinidad and Tobago.

His passion towards helping his students and people at large encouraged him to enroll at the University of the Southern Caribbean (formally called Caribbean Union College) at Maracas Valley, St Joseph. His major was Behavioural Sciences with an emphasis on psychology and sociology together with teacher training components in education.

He journeyed to Maracas Valley after work and the stress of traveling became burdensome and so Jason bought his first brand new vehicle for his birthday on January 24th 2007, so he could get that comfort of getting to work and school on time.

This made life much easier and Jason would find himself staying on campus late at nights getting his assignments done and studying to succeed at his exams. Jason started applying his knowledge in the classroom and felt that his job was less stressful. He internalized what was imparted to him at the different subjects and made it a part of his every day routine.

He would even share the knowledge with his students in the classroom as he taught during the day. Jason started to see why education was important and the true meaning of someone being educated was evident in his life. He insisted that change must start with him and believed that the greatest impact in people's lives was demonstrated through living by example. He recalled his grandmother saying to him, "The only Bible someone might be reading is your life."

In his journey however, he discovered that not all people who laugh and talk with him were true friends. This was an issue he had to deal with because he genuinely gave his best and would try to help people without looking for anything in return. Friends, family members and co-workers would say degrading and untrue things that would upset him until he discovered that the only way to combat negatives was to work harder and push himself further to succeed. He tried hard not to pay attention to their negative comments and reminded himself that Jesus was not liked when he demonstrated to man how they should live their lives.

He continued with great anticipation to achieve his goals in the short term and long term. Jason purchased his first home and moved to El Dorado. He also applied and got transferred from his "alma mata" Marbella Senior Comprehensive to South East Port of Spain Secondary School, which was located closer to his new home. This made life less stressful for Jason and he knew that better days were yet to come.

While studying Jason chose courses of interest and also those that would help him to get a greater awareness of himself and others. His study on campus was an "ah ha" experience and the terms of psychological discipline were matched with the trials he had gone through in his life.

Jason discovered that in life, if he did not work hard, he may take things for granted so he placed education as a priority and he appreciated the knowledge that was imparted. This helped him to be more effective as a teacher, in the classroom and as a person in society. "Dare to be different" was made real in his life and he saw the need in order to succeed in life. His knowledge gained at USC was used to help people to be more sensitized about life.

He found that the merging of psychology and spirituality during his first degree was fascinating and it helped him to conceptualize his experiences in life. It also helped him to realize that, as an individual, he could only do so much to help people to change but with God all things are possible. Through his studies Jason discovered his true purpose in life: he was on his way to self-actualization, as Maslow outlined in his hierarchy of needs theory.

His degree from Andrews University in Michigan USA via the University of the Southern Caribbean was helpful as he was able to advice his students and people on career choices. The merging of general education and concentration courses on campus gave him a panoramic view of education so he could help people to direct their studies in concentrated areas. His standards grew higher and he was not willing to compromise, which caused him to work harder and achieve higher. This never caused Jason to feel aloof or superior to others. Helping was a part of his nature which he was mastering at this stage in his life.

His experience on campus was bitter-sweet. He was de-motivated by a lecturer who made him complete a research and then failed him and refused to explain why he did. But being the type of individual Jason was, he decided to pursue it to get justice and, so doing, he stayed away from campus for almost a year. After persistent calls and writing letters, he was tossed about like a leaf so eventually, he let the persons who failed to deal with his issue know, that he was taking his concern to the media. The academic dean investigated the complaint. The lecturer was then disciplined and the case was solved. An "A" grade was awarded after the assignment was assessed by another lecturer on campus. Jason felt that he had an obligation to stand up for his rights as a student and to prevent other students from being abused by people in authority at the institution.

Jason continued his journey and he was awarded his bachelor degree from Andrews University in 2001. This was a great accomplishment to Jason and his family because he was the first amongst all his family and relatives to attain that level of education. This further motivated Jason to continue his education and so, after doing some research, concluded that the Nazarene College in Santa Cruz was his next institute to acquire his Master of Arts in Counseling.

While waiting to graduate formally, he started his masters in January 2002. The programme was well structured at the Nazarene College and it was the only Master of Arts in Counseling offered in Trinidad at the time. This was the area he wanted to specialize in, as a follow up from his first degree. He knew this was the right decision.

Ordained Intervention

T HROUGH FAITH JASON applied to the Nazarene College in Santa Cruz. He was the last person to be enrolled. He did not know where he was going to get money to finance the programme.

So he did what was humanly possible through faith and left the rest up to God. God again came through for Jason. He got options at different financial institutions and through the Government assisted programme, to access money to start his programme. Eventually, he finally accessed the programme. This was another sign that what he was doing was ordered by God and that he needed to continue doing what he believed God wanted him to do. Jason believed that his blessing was a result of his cycle of doing well and helping others (karma was manifested through this process). There is a saying, "What goes around comes right back around." These were words that Jason internalized and believed that would manifest eventually in one's life. Subconsciously it reminded him that if he was doing something, he should do it wholeheartedly or not at all.

While studying, Jason began to practice what was being taught to him in his programme. So he used his students as his clients and so, in a sense, he was gaining experience in the field for group, family and individual counseling. He began mentoring young boys at his school. All students, whether they were assigned to his class or not, would walk into his tailoring classroom/workshop and converse with him. Those who came to his classroom were looking for someone to talk to and more so, a male to associate with. Jason found out that many of them had absentee fathers and some of the fathers who were present were not positive role models. These students were angry and their feelings were locked up on the inside. They needed to vent their frustration; someone to listen and to advise them and to know that someone cared. He began to play the role of father to these students and it gave him great joy to see how they were willing to listen and access help.

Jason created an environment so that students could feel free to walk in and relax during the break and lunch time, and at times his classroom was packed to capacity during the lunch break. The students felt comfortable to come and sit and have their lunch. After lunch he gave permission to the students to play Scrabble and eventually the formation of a scrabble club began. He used this as an opportunity to interact and help the students to socialize in a healthy way. He coached the students and while doing so the hidden curriculum, which included, respect, manners, courtesy, fair play, manner of speech, team work and the need to appreciate one another as a human beings (uniqueness and individualism) were nurtured. When any of the students were disciplined they took it in good stride and they continued to be respectful to each other. Students knew when they entered his classroom, they would be expected to behave in a civilized manner or they would be held accountable. He was known to be strict and structured.

He felt that with the knowledge that was passed

down to him from the different courses, such as principles and theories he had learnt on campus, proved to be important tools in his classroom and even in his life. Through the interaction of the students at South East Port Of Spain Secondary School his practice began reaping results. The results were evident in the lives of these children and it gave him the incentive to continue his quest in the helping profession as a teacher and now as a brewing counseling therapist. He motivated his student and reminded them that they were special and they should treat themselves as such. Students were reminded that no matter where they came from, they had the power of choice to be successful and excel to the greatest potential that God intended them to. This was like a prayer used as a motivational lesson at the beginning of every term. At the end of the session students would say, "Thank you, sir, for reminding me of who I am and I am going to try harder to do better at my schoolwork and to become a better person." This encouraged Jason to continue to do what he was doing.

Every time he did those sessions, the students would become silent and attentive. He drew from elite leaders like Nelson Mandela and Barack Obama to concretize his beliefs. These sessions encouraged some of the students to share their problems and he began bonding with his students and creating a little family at the institution. Students looked out for one another and they looked forward to see each other, at Mr. Lugo's classroom every morning and lunch time. The students would take the key from him on mornings as he entered the compound, take his laptop bag, open up his classroom windows and positioned themselves, as though the classroom was theirs. If he stayed away from school for an important matter, he would be greatly missed and the students would let him know in no uncertain term. With the availability of his classroom as a fertile ground for empowerment, the students continued to interact with each other and they grew stronger doing positive things.

He reminded his students about their lives as being a gift and choice is a gift of life hence their choices would determine how successful they are in life. He believed in the behavioral approach and helping students to practice what is right and just. He never allowed students to belittle one another in his classes. In his classroom discipline and respect were his watch words and the code of conduct followed these guidelines, as he imparted knowledge to his students. His major concern was the majority of his students who attended the school came from high-risk communities. Neglect was a major issue and these students needed programmes to build their self-esteem, to help empower them. The need for support and attention were lacking in their lives and it was evident in their behavior.

Jason advocated for these students...made it his duty to interact with the relevant authorities including subject teachers, form teachers, the guidance counselor, parents, the principal and other supportive agents to ensure some form of support or help was issued. He advocated in whatever way he could and tried to support the students who came to him for help as he counseled on a daily basis. Jason would stay in his classroom to supervise and counsel students and neglected the comfort of an air conditioned staffroom space. He considered these children to be his own and they shared their feelings towards him through teachers' review, some spoke to their parents about the good he was doing, and by others listening to them as they defended him when someone spoke ill of Mr. Lugo. Some of the students commented on his Facebook account and BlackBerry messenger, who looked up to him as a role model:

-Kadeem Graham referred to him as his father and a role model. Who looked out for him!

-Kadeem's mother -Natalie Graham Huggins referred to him and thanked him for being a father, big brother, role model and friend when her son needed one.

Paul Dohwah referred to him as his "pops."

-Dwaine Regis referred to him as a friend and role model

-Ashland Mohamed referred to him as a friend, role model and father figure

-Josiah Thongs referred to him as a father figure who was easy to talk to and concerned about his future.

-Shakeil Regis referred to him as being cool to talk to and concerned about his grades. He looked up to Mr. Lugo as being a role model, father figure and a friend to talk to.

-Chenelle Edwards once wrote "Mr. Lugo was a teacher who stood for discipline. You knew he was concerned about the students' welfare and it was obvious in the simple things he did such as making sure students finish their class notes before leaving his class. He made it part of his business to find out what they were interested in and encouraged them to work hard at whatever they want to achieve. For instance, he knew that I was interested in fashion and wants to become a designer. He pushed me to follow my dream and advised me. He is amazing."

-Akiba Francis- "Mr. Lugo you have impacted me in the sense that you showed interest in my school success and pushed me to do my work. You reminded me not to slack off my work and make sure to study. You taught me to have equal discipline and respect towards others. I consider you to be a very intelligent person. These characteristics make me want to emulate your personality."

-Jewel referred to him as a friend, a father figure and a role model who cared about her success and aspirations in life.

-Misha Boyce-referred to him as a very cool teacher but when it comes to his work he was serious.

-Hollwin Franco Obrien —on face book remarks-Thanks a lot for everything past and present.

-Parents of his form class referred to him as caring, concerned and a disciplinarian who compelled their children to stay in order.

- In her thank you letter, Principal Mrs. Patricia Charles referred to him as "someone whose effort has not gone unnoticed for ensuring the students reach the required standards for success in his classes. Our Home-work Centre is evidence of that." I am also aware of the special interest you take in students who are at risk and your willingness to try to help." Witness; Raheem, Jetson, Jahfari among others.

It is clear that you have the interest of the children at heart and with that in mind, I would like to encourage you to further involve..."

Jason referred to these children as his sons and daughters. He developed and continued fruitful relationships with them. Students continued calling him when they needed advice and believed that his input in their lives was of great value to them.

Signs Compelled Change

J ASON WAS BOMBARDED by some co-workers who talked for talk sake but did not want to walk the walk. He felt frustrated at times with adults around him being so selfish and not willing to help the students as they were duty bound to do. This did not deter him from helping students, though, because he knew where the root of the problem originated and never blamed the students for their behaviours. During his interactions with the students he became aware that many came from homes where there were bad parenting: single parenting, selfish parents not wanting the best for their children, fatherless children, and lack of care and attention. In addition, the school curriculum, failure to address life skills and teachers who were not doing their jobs produced a cycle of unloved and hopeless citizens.

Jason felt that his purpose was to help people and was convicted without a shadow of a doubt. Jason understood through his class Career Development and Assessment, at his master's programme and through his job as a teacher, that his career path was predestined. His childhood experiences also propelled him into this career path as he would try his best to guide his clients/students in the right direction so they could live fulfilled lives.

Theorist Roe, saw the interaction of heredity

and environment as important in causing a child to develop a person or nonperson orientation, and to lead an individual to select an occupation that requires either high or low levels of interaction with others. Jason's experiences had compelled him to turn negative to positives, wrong to right and sadness to happiness. He understood how his clients could be de-motivated, ridiculed, and their reason for low self-esteem. Jason lived it all and became a victor and a testimony to encourage people to show how hard work, perseverance and believing in God can turn things around for the best. He believed that if all these elements are present in his clients' lives they can also overcome their trials.

Jason felt teaching was limiting his practice as a counseling therapist and needed to be among the best in order to become one of them. His interest shifted and he saw himself being stagnant and knew he had to move on to bigger and better things.

While he was in his final year at his master's programme, Jason decided to establish a home work centre at his school. He saw the need to target students whose parents were working late and their children were unsupervised, students who needed academic help with their homework, students who needed to develop healthy studying habits, and students who had basic reading and comprehension problems. He created an atmosphere where peer teaching could be formalized, students' grades could be monitored, there was help in career assessment and counseling was also provided.

Teachers were called upon to assist and only two external teachers gave of their time: Mrs. Little (evening class teacher) helped in the area of English for the lower forms; and Mrs. Donna Lopez (student's mother who taught English at another school). Form six students were used as mentors who assisted the children in homework and taught topics in Math.

Hollwin Obrien and Stephen Linton were only two of the students who came willingly at first, and mentored and helped the lower forms with their school work. Eventually the other students came and assisted. This was another subset of South East Port of Spain Secondary family that was established and it was interesting to see how the children develop healthy relationships in this healthy environment.

Jason took the opportunity and shared motivational topics such as life choices, time tabling, conflict resolution, time management skills and career choices. The Holland's career instrument was used to test the students so they could align themselves in the correct path by matching personality traits with career path. All of these activities were taking place while Jason was doing his studies and doing his internship hours, as a major requirement for his graduate programme, Masters in Counseling. It was not easy to balance, but he did it and did it without complaining.

In 2001 Jason's formal classroom sessions at the master's programme came to an end and he felt that he wanted to move on to the next level to become a counseling psychologist. Humanly, he was not confident to do so. He had worked hard and accomplished so much in his country that he felt it was not right to give his knowledge and expertise to another country. But he had no choice but to migrate since there was no programme in Trinidad to continue in his field at the doctorial level.

Jason's internship for his master's programme continued and his practicum had just finished at Dolly's and Associates Counselling Agency (diverse counseling and trauma hours were done). He decided to do his majority hours for his internship at Trinity East College, Trincity. Jason discovered that school counseling incorporates all types of counseling. He further developed his counselling skills and integrated different approaches. What he discovered about the usage of theories is that no one theory was considered better than the other but was used based on the clients strong or weak qualities. The use of Nouthetic (Christian) counseling continued to show its importance when academic theories failed. Cognitive, behavioral theories were the prominent ones used together when counseling with families. His experiences there further helped him to master the art in the counseling field.

Jason's experiences and his studies in the counseling field together with his practicum and internship, helped foster healing and growth in his life. Self-care was a major element that was stressed throughout the duration program of study. He conceptualized its awareness and importance and he felt good about himself. Going to the gym was scheduled once a day. Emotionally, he ensured that his friends were uplifting people who he could depend for encouragement, affirmations and support in his life and spiritually commune with God: people who were spiritually inclined, who read the Bible and who attended church for reinforcement.

The school term came to an end and so was his internship.

He took the opportunity to strengthen himself spiritually and decided to visit a co-worker's church that Sunday. He was called upon to minster in song that morning and so he did with enthusiasm, not knowing what God had planned for him. Jason felt that God spoke to him through the Pastor Ogunome that morning when he postulated that "God has everything for his children and as Christians we need to take risk, just as businessmen do in order to access our blessing."

This was a revelation for Jason and so he decided to take action through conviction on his next endeavour in life: to become one of the best in the counseling field. His courage was strengthened and he knew that with all he had been through, sacrifices were needed to be made. He made up his mind to migrate to the United States. This was difficult for him because he had to leave things behind: his car, home, job and his adopted children, friends and family.

Jason is now living in the United States of America where he has embarked on his doctoral programme in Counseling and Behavioral reform. It is his hope to work hard and to become one of the best counselor in his area of concentration. He is grateful for his experiences because they made him into the person that he is and a successful individual. Jason, as he sat and told his story with gratitude and humble attributes, emulated confidence of life achievements in his present abode. As he reminisces on his past, he is grateful for everyone who positively and negatively caused him to work harder, thus contributed to him being successful and fulfilled today. He is convinced that he is self-actualized and comfortable where he is. He continues sharing and helping people to empower themselves to become the best they can, through reaching optimum potential and so he concludes by saying "To God Be the Glory, Great Things He Has Done."

Tribute

THIS BOOK IS about Jason's experiences; his trials and triumphs throughout his life as an individual. Although the experiences may have seemed hurtful and unfair, the reasons for them happening were justified throughout his life because he became successful. Through expounded words and actions which were reveled through his studies he discovered his purpose in life. The effectiveness of his work today depicts the intensity of his struggle and through his willpower he has reached the pinnacle of success. The people whom he came into contact with in his life were no mishaps but placed at junctions to assist him with what God had ordained for him.

One of these persons whose memories Jason held close to his heart was that of a neighbor and seamstress Susan David. She had inspired him when he was at one of his lowest points in his life. Susan passed away and Jason knew he had lost a dear friend, a comforter, a teacher, and his best form of inspiration in his budding days as a tailor. As a form of comfort after her mom passed away, Jason shared with Chenell, Susan's daughter, his experiences with her mother and she was surprised to learn that her mom had such influence in his life. She expressed her heartfelt thanks to him for sharing. She actually felt some form of relief after reading this. Jason decided to include this piece of communication to Chennell, to make a point to persons to always pay tribute and never forget those individuals who made a phenomenal impact in your life.

"Be a blessing in life, not a curse!"

"Chennell your mom inspired me to go into tailoring ...I started of my career as a tailor, ended up teaching then went into counseling. God use people in our lives for different reasons. At the point when I met your mom, I was very sad and felt alone. I would leave my family and relatives who lived so close by, but who ridiculed me for my skin tone and texture of hair ...and walk to your mom's house. I would go and stare in silence as she stitched together those pieces of fabric. I was told that I won't become anything good in life. However, God used your mom to motivate me and to master a craft that he had given me as a gift. This gift God had bestowed upon me and with the assistance I got from your mom, I was able to excel at it. My self-esteem was lifted and my self-worth was built-up. God use humble people to be a blessing to others.

To cut a long story short because of that gift that was harnessed with the help of your mom, there was no turning back for this "black nigger boy' as I was referred to in those times. I became a teacher and acquired a BSc in Behavioral Science, I further went on to do a Masters (MA) in Counseling Psychology, presently pursuing another Masters in Education, as a Special Education Specialist and now doing my Doctorate in Behavioral Health. God has a way of turning things around for those who truly believe and have the faith and hope that life will get better."

Why Jason chose to be in the helping professional today... because he understands and can relate to individuals who may be experiencing similar or worse situations that he had been through. He is now focused on bringing hope to the hopeless, motivating people to become the best that they can be and to continue exploring his God given talents. His position as an Education Specialist, where he has the task of dealing with the most vulnerable students in that district, gives him such pleasure, and the assurance deep in his heart, that this is what God was preparing him for all along. God has a way of raising people up who are sincere, genuine and who are willing to obey his command throughout life. Choose to be a blessing or a curse!

Therapeutic Work Sheet

ONE OF JASON'S main objective in writing this book was to influence the reader to empower themselves and so doing empower others. By so doing he has outlined a simple therapeutic assessment sheet at the back of the book. This will give an individual a good sense of where and who you are now or where you want to reach in life. It is simple and possible and if taken seriously and honestly can help alleviate problems in life that can cause you to be stagnated or stunted.

This can be used as an assessment for you and others around you so it can give you a sense of guidance to where you are and what is required for you to move forward in life. It is an integrated approach in counseling and has the psychoanalysis, here and now and existentialism approaches in the therapeutic attempt to help you the reader, assess your life. If you are having difficulty to assess and if you realize that you are psychologically disturbed after the assessment, it is imperative for you to seek professional help. Counseling therapists who are licensed should be equipped to help you get control of your life. It will require your willingness to get help and for you to do the necessary work.

You have the power to change things and so doing can do wonders in the reformation of one's life and others around you. Life has many challenges and some of us need that extra push and support. But it is imperative that you acknowledge that you need help and is willing to do the necessary work to change things around you. Starting with self and wanting the best out of life is a start. When the tools of empowerment are utilized changes can take place from the inside out. Jason is living proof of enhancing the changes that accompany empowerment and he believes that all human beings have that power within themselves to do great things. Deep seated belief in one's ability transferred into action can open up a whole new world of hidden talents and gifts which were bestowed upon you as a human being. The discovery and utilization of your inborn talents and gifts can guarantee your dreams of a better life being fulfilled.

You are what you are predestined by your dominating thoughts. Your actions fostered by "will power" will ultimately get you where you want to go. It was great joy to share my experience and knowledge to help you to empower yourself.

Good luck and stay strong!

Best,

Jason Lugo.

Appendix 1

B ASIC GUIDED QUESTIONS an individual can answer to determine if they are indeed heading towards their full potential. If the individual cannot answer or believe that the questions are too tough to answer, brings up hurt, causes them not to move on, this is an indication for the individual to see a therapist…this is an indication that the individual needs help to overcome the problem from the past or at present.

NB: It is imperative for the client to be honest with self if change has to take place.

- Is there anything that continues to make you uncomfortable from your childhood? Please give a short explanation.

- ....
....
....
....

- How do you feel about the situation at present?

- ....
....
....
....

- Does the problem keep coming up and interrupts your plans?

- ....
....
....
....

- Do you have any idea how you can overcome this?

- ....

....

....

....

- How do you feel about self?

- ....

....

....

....

- Is there anything you would like to change in your life at present?

- ....

....

....

....

- Now that you have identified the change you would like to have in your life, how do you plan to effect this change?

- ....

....

....

....

- Do you have any plans for the future concerning your Life, career, feelings, relationship, etc.?

- ....
....
....
....

- What are you doing to make those plans a reality?

- ....
....
....
....

- Is it working?

- ....
....
....
....

- Should you make a new plan and what would it involve?

- ....
....
....
....

Printed in the United States
By Bookmasters